An Artistic Tribute to Harriet Tubman

By the Same Authors

JULIA C. DAVIS

Empowering English Language Learners: Successful Strategies of Christian Educators (contributing author)

Keeping the Dream Alive: A Reflection on the Art of Harriet Lorence Nesbitt (contributing author)

Specialist Fourth Class John Joseph DeFazio: Advocating for Disabled American Veterans (contributing author)

JEANNE C. DeFAZIO

Creative Ways to Build Christian Community (edited with John P. Lathrop)

How to Have an Attitude of Gratitude on the Night Shift (with Teresa Flowers)

Redeeming the Screens: Living Stories of Media "Ministers" Bringing the Message of Jesus Christ to the Entertainment Industry (edited with William David Spencer)

Berkeley Street Theatre: How Improvisation and Street Theater Emerged as Christian Outreach to the Culture of the Time (editor)

Empowering English Language Learners: Successful Strategies of Christian Educators (edited with William David Spencer)

Keeping the Dream Alive: A Reflection on the Art of Harriet Lorence Nesbitt (author and editor)

Specialist Fourth Class John Joseph DeFazio: Advocating for Disabled American Veterans (editor)

An Artistic Tribute to Harriet Tubman

JULIA C. DAVIS
JEANNE C. DEFAZIO
EDITORS

Afterword by Wilma Faye Mathis

RESOURCE *Publications* • Eugene, Oregon

AN ARTISTIC TRIBUTE TO HARRIET TUBMAN

Resource Publications
An Imprint of Wipf and Stock Publishers
199 W. 8th Ave., Suite 3
Eugene, OR 97401

www.wipfandstock.com

PAPERBACK ISBN: 978-1-7252-8478-4
HARDCOVER ISBN: 978-1-7252-8479-1
EBOOK ISBN: 978-1-7252-8480-7

01/12/21

This book is dedicated to Harriet Tubman. As a leading abolitionist, she brought black slaves to freedom during the nineteenth century. She was the "Moses" of the enslaved African American. Her legacy continues to inspire people of every race to find the leader within themselves. Harriet's exemplary faith in God empowered generations of African Americans to restore their own lives and through Christian outreach to liberate others. Her great faith extends to all of us. In Harriet's words: "I said to the Lord, I'm going to hold steady on to you, and I know you will see me through."[1]

—Jeanne DeFazio

1. "Harriet Tubman—I said to de Lord, 'I'm goin' to hold. . ." https://www.brainyquote.com/quotes/harriet_tubman_629150.

Contents

Foreword

In the winter of 2020, I came up with the idea to publish digital images of original art representing the life of Harriet Tubman. Julia C. Davis and Wilma Faye Mathis agreed to write this book. Both of these women contribute to this work a lifetime of understanding how to overcome challenges. As African American women, this team of authors, educators, and inner-city African American church leaders came together to build a bridge across the racial divide and promote reconciliation.

> Last Memorial Day, May 25, 2020, [an African American] George Floyd died during his arrest for potentially stealing a pack of cigarettes. As a result, protests and riots have been occurring throughout the United States. While Floyd was being arrested, the arrest process was filmed not only by the store camera but by bystanders.[2]
>
> It's painful that these murders occurred during a pandemic that is disproportionately threatening and destroying the livelihoods and lives of African Americans, Hispanic Americans, and other minority communities. Tens of millions have lost their jobs, and hundreds of thousands have lost family, friends, and loved ones.[3]

2. Spencer and Spencer, "Responding to Floyd Killing," lines 10–13.
3. Shah, "Reflecting on Violence against African Americans," lines 19–22.

Julia and Wilma, like Harriet Tubman, overcame racial injustice. Their ministries have promoted interracial healing because they understand the six degrees of separation implicit in Martin Luther King Jr.'s words, "We may have all come on different ships, but we're in the same boat now."[4]

As a contributing author to *Empowering English Language Learners*, Julia Davis explains why and how she taught Christian principles, particularly forgiveness without retribution, in a politically correct fashion for the inner-city public school system:

> Scripturally based Classroom Rules are a way to bring the practice of Christian principle into the public school classroom without being "politically incorrect." My students begin each class by devising classroom principles. When students have written the Classroom Rules, they are more apt to abide by them. For example, "I am ready to be respectful and responsible and a good classroom citizen" reflects the values of Psalm 19:14, Proverbs 18:24 and Mark 12:31. "Listening without interrupting" describes the wisdom of Proverbs 18:2. "Speaking without accusing" is a mandate of James 1:19. "Answering without arguing" is an instruction of Proverbs 17:1. Ephesians 4:15 outlines the importance of "sharing." "Forgiveness without retribution" is a mandate of Colossians 3:13.[5]

In *Empowering English Language Learners*, Wilma Faye Mathis explains how important faith and the application of God's Word are to enhance the mind of students:

> The first thing I assure my students is that I will walk alongside you, be there to help you to organize, get through assignments, and brainstorm. But most of all, I will lift you up and call your name in prayer, asking that God will anoint and illuminate the faculty of your minds, until you gain a better understanding now and in your own continued studies. In the modern and this post-modern day, men and women have faced a lot of stress at work, home, ministry, and in school. But I am there

4. Martin Luther King Jr., at Brainy Quotes.
5. DeFazio and Spencer, *Empowering English Language Learners*, 40.

> to remind the students that Christ is the source of their strength, refreshment, and peace, and to remember: "Whatever you do, do it enthusiastically, as something done for the Lord and not for people" (Col. 3:23).[6]

These women are the legacy of Harriet Tubman. Thomas Garrett once said of her (Harriet Tubman), "I never met with any person of any color who had more confidence in the voice of God, as spoken directly to her soul."[7] Julia and Wilma share with Harriet Tubman a relationship of intimacy with God and Jesus' wisdom, which empowers both of them to accomplish the tasks set before them.

JEANNE DEFAZIO

6. DeFazio and Spencer, *Empowering English Language Learners*, 91–92.
7. "Harriet Tubman and the Underground Railroad," lines 44-48.

Acknowledgments

Editing this book has been my privilege and honor. I want to thank Dr. William David Spencer for reading the manuscript and making helpful suggestions. Thanks to Bridget Long, PhD, Dean of the Harvard Graduate School of Education, for role-modeling racial equity. President Theresa Rodgers empowers all her students at St. Francis High School to make a difference. My wonderful niece Ella Louise Ryan for showing me how to Zoom during the 2020 pandemic. Governor Jerry Brown for creating the Oakland Military Institute to develop leadership among youth of every race and color. Gemma Wenger for being an inspiration as an inner-city educator. Aaron Mann, who gave me wonderful professional advice through this process. Jozy Pollock and Mel Novak for decades of chaplaincy and rehabilitation of incarcerated people of every color. Billie Hemphill for her discernment. Missionary Gloria Harris for her support of this project. Linda Lockhart for reminding me to trust in Jesus. Pastor Judith Kang for leading me closer to God. Teresa Flowers for her prayers. Charlene Eber for her kind words. Jimmie Borders for founding Fueled by Prayer. Louise Maguire for her continued support and guidance. Mary Ciarcia for her humor. Donna Louise Thayer for being a devoted educator who empowered children of all races. Dr. Jan Murray Garcia, MD, and Dr. Michael Reed, MD, for their dedication as physicians during the 2020 pandemic.

University of California Chancellor May has done a stellar job adapting the Davis campus to suit the need of the student body during the pandemic. Dan Arnerich, who helped me keep going. Thanks to Caleb Loring III for supporting this work. I am indebted to Peter Lynch for his kindness. Most of all, I thank Jesus for giving me the strength to carry on.

Jeanne DeFazio

An Artistic Tribute to Harriet Tubman

Julia C. Davis

I GREW UP UNDER the influence of a Bible-believing mother who maintained that Scripture is historically accurate, inerrant, and fully authoritative as the Word of God. In daily prayer, my mother put God in remembrance of the promises in his Word. She believed that God "hath made of one blood all nations of men for to dwell on all the face of the earth" (Acts 17:26). I learned how to pray from hearing my mother cry out to the Lord. She pleaded with God for all humans to receive Jesus' gift of redemptive love and God's forgiveness. Like Harriet Tubman, my mother shared daily communion with God. Rebecca Janney sums up Harriet Tubman's spiritual impact:

> The power of Harriet Tubman's life was rooted in her constant communion and intimacy with Jesus through the Holy Spirit as she fought against injustice and served others. As someone testified about her, "Her relations with the Deity were personal, even intimate, though respectful on her part. Harriet Tubman lived a life of intimacy with Jesus and wisdom that empowered her to accomplish the tasks set before her."[1]

1. Janney, *Harriet Tubman*, 62.

Robert Gudmestad explains:

> What I find most fascinating, as a historian of American slavery, is how belief in God helped Tubman remain fearless, even when she came face to face with many challenges.[2]

As an educator, I understand how important it is for African Americans to know their history. Frederick Douglass wrote, "Some men know the value of education by having it. I know its value by not having it."[3] In my research I found evidence to suggest that Harriet Tubman stopped at Frederick Douglass's home.[4] Douglass wrote a letter honoring Tubman's work.[5]

On Martin Luther King Jr. Day, 2019, I attended the Harvard Divinity School's Andover-Harvard Theological Library exhibit, "The Yoke of Bondage: Christianity and African Slavery in the United States."[6] It contained documents that enlightened me about my ancestors' experience in slavery.[7] Those documents and artifacts give a fifth dimension to the racist reality of the nineteenth-century African American slave. Structural racism cannot be ignored.

> . . . structural racism continues to disproportionately segregate communities of color from access to opportunity and upward mobility by making it more difficult for people of color to secure quality education, jobs, housing, healthcare, and equal treatment in the criminal justice system.[8]
>
> I've seen a lot of that and I know a lot of that to be true. It's not something you're meant to talk about in

2. Gudmestad, "Faith Made Harriet Tubman Fearless," lines 5–7.
3. Douglass, "Blessings of Liberty and Education," lines 1–2.
4. Clinton, *Harriet Tubman*, 84.
5. Humez, *Harriet Tubman*, 306–7.
6. See "Yoke of Bondage."
7. See Davis, "Yoke of Bondage."
8. "Structural Racism in America."

> There is a oneness of physical structure, of conditions and modes of life, of possible or actual development, which forbids any one race or nation, Hebrew, Hellenic, Latin, or Teutonic, to assume for itself that it is the cream and flower of humanity.[13]

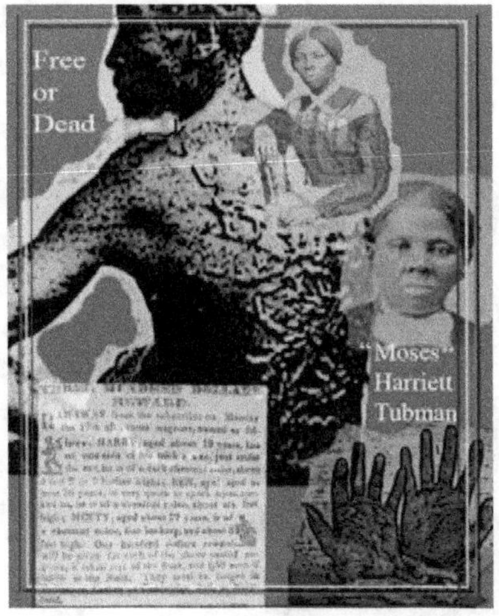

The Price of Freedom
Olga Soler

This artwork is entitled "The Price of Freedom." As the story goes Harriet Tubman was whipped 5 times for falling asleep while on the job of rocking the cradle of a white baby. She was also said to hold a gun to the head of any slave that lost their nerve once they were on the road to freedom. A human being should not have to make such choices to live like a human being. But if a child can't fall asleep in peace then the price of freedom high as it is must be paid.[14]

13. Ellicot, *Bible Commentary for English Readers*, on Acts 17:26, quoted from https://biblehub.com/commentaries/acts/17-26.htm.

14. Olga Soler, email to Jeanne DeFazio, June 14, 2020.

The Price of Freedom combines early daguerreotypes of Harriet Tubman with a digital image of bounty on her head as a runaway slave. Olga fills her background with an image of a black female body in physical pain. *The Price of Freedom* is the artist's warning against the cost of racism. Olga understands that racism is human bondage designed by the Adversary and demonic emissaries sent to do divisionary work. She embraces Martin Luther King Jr.'s dream that all God's children will one day live in peace, unity, harmony, and joy (John 14:27; Romans 14:17).

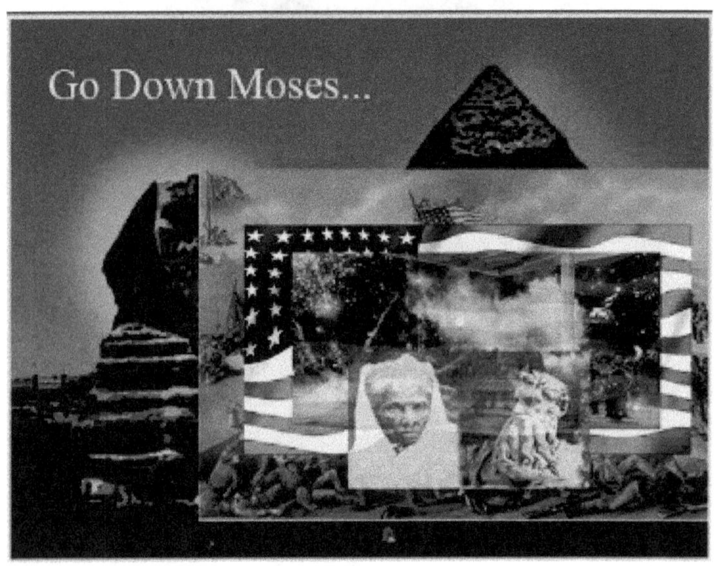

Go Down Moses
Olga Soler

"Go Down Moses" is the African American-spiritual that describes the events in Exodus 8:1: "And the LORD spake unto Moses, Go unto Pharaoh, and say unto him, Thus saith the LORD, Let my people go, that they may serve me" (KJV). The Egyptian pyramids in the backdrop represent Pharaoh's abuse of Israelite slaves. A photo of Harriet Tubman next to Michelangelo's statue of the biblical patriarch identifies Harriet as Moses' female counterpart.

The Civil War rages on at the bottom of this artwork and the American flag is flying high for freedom and equality at the top the middle image of present unrest tells us racial freedom is still a work in progress that we must urgently continue to address. When Harriet Tubman died in 1913, the American flag was placed over her casket. She was buried with semi-military honors at Fort Hill Cemetery in Auburn, New York, because of her patriotic service in the Union Army.[15] Her gravestone is inscribed, "Servant of God, Well Done."[16]

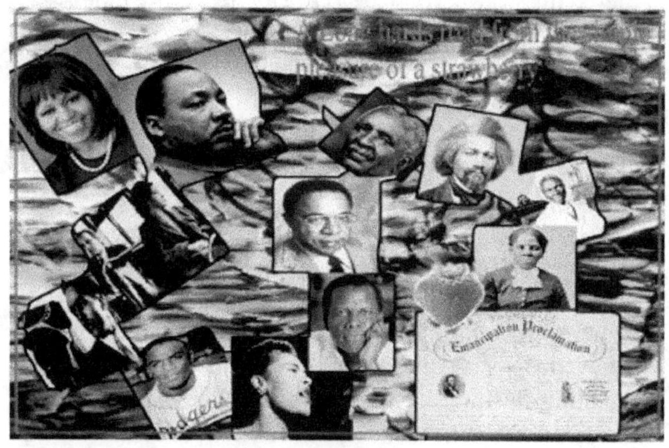

A Long Hard Road from the Simple Pleasure of a Strawberry
Olga Soler

Olga's collage is a photo feast of African American icons who are all the legacy of Harriet Tubman:

> Sojourner Truth—poet "And Ain't I a Woman" and abolitionist, Fredrick Douglas, George Washington Carver—scientist, Alex Hailey—author of "Roots," Sidney Portier—actor, Billy Holiday—Jazz singer- who sang "Strange Fruit" about lynching, Jackie Robinson—one of the first black baseball players to play on a white team, Langston Hugues—poet, Rosa Parks—arrested during the civil

15. Clinton, *Harriet Tubman*, 216.
16. "Harriet Tubman Grave," line 9.

> rights movement for sitting on the white side of the bus, Martin Luther King Jr. and First Lady Michelle Obama.[17]

Central to the composition is a strawberry symbolizing the miracle-working power of Jesus' blood coursing through Harriet's life:

> By the 1300s, it is common to find strawberries pictured in Italian, Flemish and German art as well as in English miniatures as a symbol of perfect righteousness. Why? Because, the *Symbol-Fibel* tells us, medieval man believed the strawberry to be a cure for depressive illnesses; thus, its presence suggests the healing powers of Christ that lead us to eternal salvation.[18]

The strawberry on top of the Emancipation Proclamation is symbolic. George Darrow, in his work *The Strawberry: History, Breeding, and Physiology*, explains:

> [The strawberry] . . . stands for noble thought and modesty, for although it is conspicuous by its color and fragrance, it nevertheless bows humbly to the earth.' Its three-partitioned leaf is a reminder of the Holy Trinity. The fruits, pointing downward, are the drops of Blood of Christ, and the five petals of its white flower, His five Wounds.[19]

The strawberry was reported to be Harriet Tubman's favorite fruit.[20] As Olga explains:

> A small thing like strawberries might have delighted the life of a woman like Harriet Tubman and been a mitigating influence sent from God to ease her life of danger and suffering. This was something that enabled her to free slaves whose children's children have filled the world with justice.[21]

17. Interview by email, Olga Soler, July 16, 2020.

18. Jordan, "Strawberry," lines 50–59.

19. Darrow, *Strawberry*, 13.

20. The "Harriet Tubman Strawberry Stroll . . . is an annual event in Auburn organized by The Harriet Tubman Boosters that celebrates Harriet Tubman through one of her favorite treats." "Harriet Tubman Strawberry Stroll," lines 4–6.

21. Interview by email, Olga Soler, July 17, 2020.

Olga places the strawberry, representing the Godhead, on top of the Emancipation Proclamation because the edict invoked the favor of God.

> And upon this act, sincerely believed to be an act of justice, warranted by the Constitution, upon military necessity, I invoke the considerate judgment of mankind, and the gracious favor of Almighty God.[22]

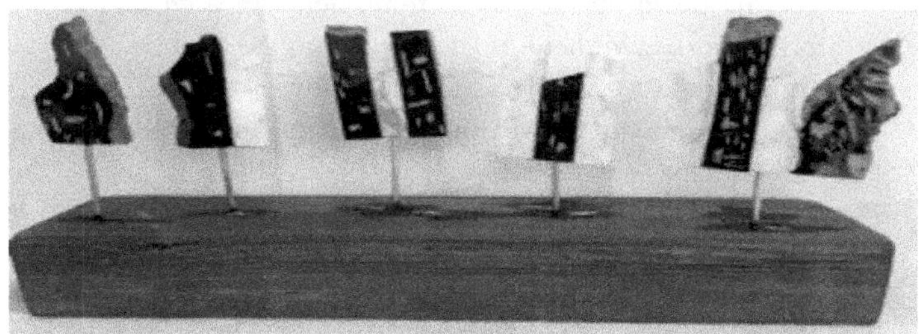

Who Were You? Who Are You? Who Do You Want to Be?
Tony Gangitano

> My primary experience with diversity and inclusion is through the addition of an African American Cuban sister-in-law and her family, a mixed-race nephew, and a mixed-race grandson. Initial reactions from both families ranged from welcoming to accepting to prejudicial. Over the years as the two families included each other in celebrations and holiday events, the mix is working. One highlight was the honor to participate as the Elder of my family at my nephew's Nigerian wedding ritual. This piece represents my observation of part of the African American experience. What I call the questioning of stages of personal identity. This is a progression of seeing oneself as a separate individual/race/culture a part of an ever-increasing mixed race/culture/society while maintaining our individuality and diverse perspectives.[23]

22. "Transcript of the Proclamation," lines 34–35.
23. Interview by email, Tony Gangitano, July 15, 2020.

It is my impression that the artist uses black and white vertical lines, creating an abstract of interracial family harmony where love blurs the color line and binds the human family. In the wake of George Floyd's death and in the 2020 racial riots, I feel this is a prayer calling God into remembrance of his promise of the New Jerusalem:

> Then I saw a new heaven and a new earth, for the first heaven and the first earth had passed away, and the sea was no more. And I saw the holy city, new Jerusalem, coming down out of heaven from God, prepared as a bride adorned for her husband. And I heard a loud voice from the throne saying, "Behold, the dwelling place of God is with man. He will dwell with them, and they will be his people, and God himself will be with them as their God. He will wipe away every tear from their eyes, and death shall be no more, neither shall there be mourning, nor crying, nor pain anymore, for the former things have passed away." And he who was seated on the throne said, "Behold, I am making all things new." Also he said, "Write this down, for these words are trustworthy and true." (Revelation 21:1–5 ESV)

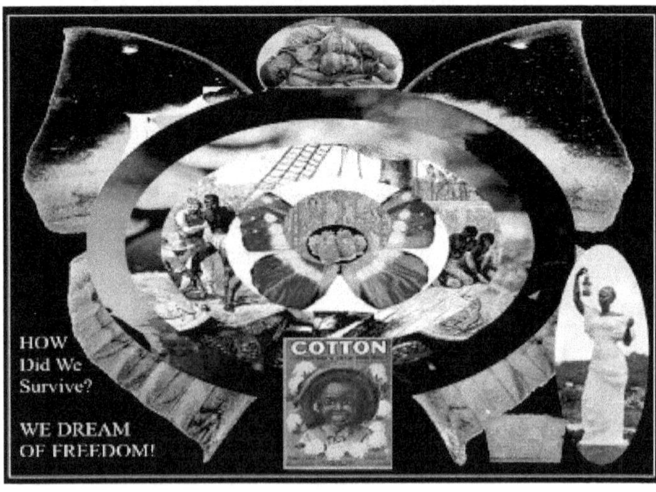

How Did We Survive? We Dreamed of Freedom
Olga Soler

Olga created this dream sequence as an antidote for suffering. On the medieval panel in the center of this collage is a snake on the cross. The snake on the cross in medieval art symbolizes the healing power of Jesus. In Numbers 21:9 the Israelites rebel against God.

> God sends poisonous serpents as punishment, but provides a bronze serpent on a pole so that a person who had been bitten could "look at the serpent of bronze and live."[24]

Jesus references Numbers 21:9, identifying his experience of crucifixion with the snake being lifted up on the pole, foreshadowing his act of salvation:

> as Moses lifted up the serpent in the wilderness, even so the Son of Man must be lifted up. That whosoever believes in him shall not perish but have eternal Life. (John 3:14–15)

Olga added strawberries to the heart of the collage to identify healing as a gift of the Holy Spirit, described by Paul the apostle in 1 Corinthians 12:9: "The same Spirit gives great faith to another, and to someone else the one Spirit gives the gift of healing."

> The strawberry is the symbol of perfect righteousness, or the emblem of the righteous man whose fruits are good works. When shown with other fruits and flowers, it represents the good works of the righteous or the fruits of the Holy Spirit.[25]

Images of the enslaved African American dreaming of freedom while working cotton fields surround the strawberries and the medieval relief as a reminder that God's mercy is poured out on suffering humankind through Jesus' act of salvation. This dream sequence is a prayer for healing, putting God in remembrance of the promises in his Word:

> If my people, which are called by my name, shall humble themselves, and pray, and seek my face, and turn

24. "Numbers 21:4–9—The Bronze Serpent," lines 1–2.

25. "Signs and Symbols," lines 281–83.

> from their wicked ways; then will I hear from heaven, and will forgive their sin, and will heal their land. (2 Chronicles 7:14)

I can't thank Olga and Tony enough for their multi-textural tribute to Harriet Tubman. They are masters of composition, using color and line to show us what is important through the lens of Harriet Tubman's life. Tony's *Mother Africa—Wet Nurse Diaspora* and Olga's *The Price of Freedom* expose the abuse of slavery, explaining the way not to behave. Olga's *Go Down Moses* shows us how we should behave. Tony's *Who Were You? Who Are You? Who Do You Want to Be?*, full of brotherly love and inclusion, shows us how life should be. Olga's *How Did We Survive? We Dreamed of Freedom* and *A Long Hard Road from the Simple Pleasure of a Strawberry* identify the miracle-working power of Jesus to transform every life. As William David Spencer explains:

> As the center of hope in a world gone awry, the promise of grace, embodied the hope of reconciling humanity to the redeeming God, as he was given as God's gift to lead and inspire us all to do works of mercy and reconciliation.[26]

I chose to author *An Artistic Tribute to Harriet Tubman* as a reminder that we, like Harriet, are called to be voices to prepare the way for Jesus' return.

> We too are called to be voices, temporary voices which God will use to prepare the way in our generation. We are the voice for this time and for this place. Our role is temporary, but it is essential. Without the voice, people will not hear.[27]

26. DeFazio, *Keeping the Dream Alive*, 27.

27. Vryhof, "Nativity of John the Baptist," lines 228–35.

Afterword

Wilma Faye Mathis

Growing up and hearing about Harriet Tubman, I was always connected to her involvement in the Underground Railroad. Although this was very significant, after reading about Tubman in Catherine Clinton's book, watching the movie *Harriet*, and most recently taking a virtual tour through the Harriet Tubman Underground Railroad Visitor Center,[28] I discovered much more. As an African American woman, I am delighted to echo my sentiments to the woman Harriet Tubman, who fought and sacrificed to abolish slavery in the nineteenth century so that they may experience freedom, which extends now to all black and brown people in this present generation to experience the freedom from the racism and injustices that continue to hang over their heads. The motto Tubman left as part of her legacy says, "if you are tired, keep going; if you are scared, keep going, if you are hungry keep going; if you want freedom, keep going."[29] Tubman made many contributions that extended beyond leading slaves to freedom. Although illiterate,[30] Tubman was a scout under the secretary of war. In this capacity, she was granted a pass to travel from the North to the South to

28. See "Harriet Tubman Underground Railroad Visitor Center."

29. Clinton, *Harriet Tubman,* 221.

30. "Illiterate, but deeply religious." Clinton, *Harriet Tubman,* 2.

help coordinate and assist the Union Army.[31] Tubman was also a nurse, caring for the countless people who were wounded. "This was a high honor and one that had not been granted to a black woman thus far."[32]

Tubman suffered a severe head injury as she stepped between a lead weight thrown by a store owner and the slave for whom it was meant. She recovered but suffered debilitating episodes for the rest of her life. Following this tragic incident, Tubman began receiving visions from God. She "had been visited by powerful visions, walking dreams that she felt were sending her messages."[33] She had great faith and combined it with action.[34] There is no wonder Tubman was named the "Moses" of the nineteenth century. She saw firsthand the ugliness of slavery and how it tore families apart. She used her visions, like Moses, who delivered the Israelites from slavery, to go and free her people. Here stands a brave, resilient, perseverant, no-nonsense kind of a woman who beat the odds, delivered both slaves and her family members from slavery, and led them to freedom. She desired freedom for all as she said, "I have heard their groans and sighs, and seen their tears, and I would give every drop of blood in my veins to free them."[35]

We can build a connection to Harriet Tubman and her life. In our present generation, there are arising Harriet Tubmans. She was a normal person, born into slavery, illiterate, but she did amazing things despite the odds against her, letting us know that we can too. There are black and brown people today who are relentless and have made the conscious decision to fight and not give up: men fighting for a better life, women making sacrifices for their children to ensure they will become a better generation, youth determined not to become a statistic, entrepreneurs with big dreams, little to work with, but taking risks. In the middle of the 2020 pandemic, we have witnessed many lives taken by the coronavirus, and protest

31. Clinton, *Harriet Tubman*, 186–87.

32. Clinton, *Harriet Tubman*, 187.

33. Clinton, *Harriet Tubman*, 29.

34. Clinton, *Harriet Tubman*, 31.

35. Bradford, *Scenes in the Life of Harriet Tubman*, 14.

marches stimulated from the tragic death of another black man, George Floyd. In these marches across the world, we were able to see people young, old, black, white, and multi-ethnic united together with a single focus—justice! It was Martin Luther King Jr. who said of certain basic First Amendment privileges that he had read of "the freedom of assembly . . . freedom of speech . . . and the freedom of the press. But he also read that the greatness of America is the right to protest for right."[36] This is why I can agree with Julia Davis in standing for racial equity, where every person should be treated as a human being and not better or worse depending on the color of their skin. Harriet Tubman resonated with the heart of God and believed in freedom: "God's time is always near, He set the Morning Star in the heavens; He gave me the strength in my limbs; He meant I should be free."[37] Freedom is against structural racism, which is defined as:

> A system in which public policies, institutional practices, cultural representations, and other norms work in various, often reinforcing ways to perpetuate racial group inequity. It identifies dimensions of our history and culture that have allowed privileges associated with "whiteness" and disadvantages associated with "color" to endure and adapt over time. Structural racism is not something that a few people or institutions choose to practice. Instead it has been a feature of the social, economic and political systems in which we all exist.[38]

As a Bible scholar, I believe in the Scriptures, which do not promote racism, but boldly state: "There is neither Jew nor Gentile, neither slave nor free, nor is there male and female, for you are all one in Christ Jesus" (Galatians 3:28). In honor of Harriet Tubman, a superior advocate who relentlessly stayed the course in her fight against slavery, the fight for equality and freedom from discrimination continues. Our black and brown people are more determined

36 "How Dr. King Cited the Constitution," lines 17–20.

37. Tubman to Ednah Dow Cheney, New York City, circa 1859; see "Quotes."

38. "11 Terms You Should Know," lines 1–17.

than ever to have justice for all! Tubman was selfless, and as she approached the latter days of her life and was asked to give a speech, it included these words: "I did not take up the work for my own benefit, but for those of my race who need help. The work is now well started and I know God will raise up others to take care of the future."[39]

39. Clinton, *Harriet Tubman*, 210.

About the Authors

JULIA C. DAVIS

Julia Davis, earned an EdM from the Harvard Graduate School of Education, and an EdM from Bouve College of Health Sciences at Northeastern University. She has held teaching certificates in New York, Massachusetts, and the District of Columbia and has been certified as an Assistant Principal and as an Assistant Special Education Supervisor. Julia has taught in the public and private sector in community-based programs including METCO, Summer STEP opportunities for underrepresented populations in science and technology, and Head Start. She has served as a member of the Parents' Advocacy Group for Massachusetts, supporting FAPE and mainstreaming special education students. She has taught pre-K through twelfth grade, adult non-readers, limited English language learners, and GED preparation courses. Julia taught internationally as an undergraduate exchange student in a special education program based in Newnham on Severn, Gloucestershire, England, which operated under the auspices of Antioch College in Ohio. Julia and her husband, Dan, have three children and three grandchildren. They attend the International Family Church in North Reading, Massachusetts. Julia developed a monthly prayer breakfast program for the Everett, Massachusetts, community.[1]

1. See DeFazio and Spencer, *Empowering English Language Learners*, 150–51.

JEANNE DEFAZIO

Jeanne DeFazio is a SAG/AFTRA (Screen Actors Guild—American Federation of Television and Radio Artists) actress of Spanish/Italian descent, who played supporting parts in theater, movies, and television series and disappeared into a life of service to the marginalized in the drama of real life. Jeanne became a teacher of second-language-learner children in the barrios of San Diego. A woman of great faith, intelligence, and energy, she completed a Bachelor of Arts in history at the University of California, Davis, pursued seminary education at Gordon-Conwell Theological Seminary (MAR, theology), and completed a Cal State TEACH English-language-learners program. Since 2009, Jeanne has returned as an Athanasian Teaching Scholar at Gordon-Conwell's multicultural Boston Center for Urban Ministerial Education (CUME), which serves the often unnoticed but thriving ethnic churches.[2]

WILMA FAYE MATHIS

Wilma Faye Mathis serves on the ministerial board in her local church, New Life Restoration Temple, Boston, Massachusetts. Wilma has served the church in many capacities and is currently the Christian Education Director, Women's Department Vice President in her national organization, and visionary for Mom 2 Mom, a single moms ministry. Professionally, Wilma is a project manager and entrepreneur. She holds a Master of Arts in urban ministry and a Master of Divinity, and serves as Teaching Assistant in systematic theology at Gordon-Conwell Theological Seminary, Boston, Massachusetts, while currently pursuing her Doctor of Ministry at Knox Theological Seminary, Fort Lauderdale, Florida. Wilma also finds time to volunteer at homeless shelters for women, providing a safe space of encouragement and transformation in the company of Christians. She is an avid Bible scholar and counts it a privilege to teach and preach the Word of God. She is a proud mom, loves the Lord, and avails herself to be used for God's glory

2. Spencer and Spencer, "Christian Egalitarian Leadership", xi.

as she echoes the words of the psalmist: "Teach me, O Lord, the way of thy statutes; and I shall keep it unto the end. Give me understanding, and I shall keep thy law; yea, I shall observe it with my whole heart" (Psalm 119:33–34).

About the Artists

TONY GANGITANO

Tony was born in Brooklyn, New York. He received a Bachelor of Science in landscape architecture from the University of Georgia and returned to work in New York City. He moved to San Diego, California, to study art. Independent study/travel in many countries led Tony to Italy, where he lived and worked as a sculptor for two years. He interned in ceramic and bronze with sculptor Alberto Ricci in Rome, then did internships and independent study of stone carving at Studio Sem and bronze casting at Tommasi Foundry, both in Pietra Santa, Italy. Upon returning to California, he pursued a Master of Fine Arts at San Diego State University. There the love of carving stone and casting bronze took a back seat to less traditional materials, which he incorporated into more conceptual sculptures and site-specific installations. Tony's work has been exhibited in group shows, two-person shows, and featured artist shows in Europe and the United States. He is a creative, high-energy, conceptually oriented mixed media sculptor. He resides in San Diego, California. His current work is fresh and exciting, incorporating thoughtful concepts and new materials.

> Fine Art is my first language. I was fortunate to be raised by a father, and grandfathers who were artist and creative craftsman, and a mother who excused my eccentric behavior by saying in a Brooklyn accent, "Its ok . . . he's and awwwtist." My work is about the integration of aesthetic

> form and emotional and intellectual content. The evolution of my art has progressed on confluent paths. Traditional figurative merged with abstract style in stone, bronze, resin, foam, and often incorporating conceptual mixed media elements. I employ archetypal images that communicate the essential commonalities of our human condition and experience. These images, combined with the juxtaposition and dialog created between figures, shapes, and materials, provoke visual, visceral, and intellectual interaction with the viewer.[3]

OLGA SOLER

Olga Soler is director/writer and performer for Estuary Ministries, a Christ-centered performing arts ministry dealing with biblical themes, inner healing, abuse, and addictive problems. The art forms used include drama, dance, storytelling, mime, comedy, graphic arts, writing, film, and song. Olga attended the High School of Performing Arts ("Fame"), the Lee Strasberg Theater Institute, and the Herbert Berghof Studios, in New York City. She has performed widely at conferences, churches, prisons, coffee houses, support groups, youth groups, and retreats and has even performed on the streets, at secular colleges, and in worship services across the United States and the United Kingdom. She holds degrees in education and communications with equivalent studies in theology and psychology. She studied for two years at Gordon Conwell Theological Seminary. She has designed and conducted the workshops "Dance Alive" and "Trauma Drama" at many Christian recovery conferences. She wrote the curriculum for and conducted discovery groups for addicts at the Boston Rescue Mission, using the arts to help them process aspects of their recovery. She also conducts workshops for Christian drama and dance in many churches of all denominations. Using Paulo Freire's *Pedagogy of the Oppressed*, she wrote a script for the Mosaics group of parents, helping their children who were victims of sexual abuse through

3. Tony Gangitano, email to Jeanne DeFazio, July 18, 2020.

the courts system and assisted them in filming the script for a documentary. She performed and coauthored scripts for four years with the Christian ministry named Team in Massachusetts and conducted eight full-scale multimedia presentations out of the Rio Ondo Arts Place in Woburn, Massachusetts, including *Voice of the Martyrs*, *Techno Easter*, and *Clean Comedy Night*. She has directed and choreographed entire productions at universities and colleges, including *A Man for All Seasons*, *Jane Eyre*, *Amal and the Night Visitors*, and (by permission of the author) Calvin Miller's *The Singer*. She wrote and illustrated the book *Epistle to the Magadalenes* and has conducted retreats for women using the book accompanied by dramatic presentation. She is the author of many other books and assorted screenplays. She is the proud mother of three wonderful children, Cielo, Reva, and Ransom. She lives in Massachusetts with her husband, Chris, and her Japanese Chin (dog), Kiji.[4]

Email: fleursavag@yahoo.com

4. See DeFazio, *Keeping the Dream Alive*, 32–33.

Bibliography

"11 Terms You Should Know to Better Understand Structural Racism." Aspen Institute, July 11, 2016. https://www.aspeninstitute.org/blog-posts/structural-racism-definition/.

"African Diaspora." *Wikipedia*. https://en.wikipedia.org/wiki/African_diaspora.

Ajayi, Ade J. F., ed. *General History of Africa*, vol. 6, *Africa in the Nineteenth Century until the 1880s*. Paris: United Nations Educational, Scientific and Cultural Organization (UNESCO), 1998.

"Always remember, you have within you the strength, the patience and the passion to reach for the stars to change the world." *Philosiblog*, August 10, 2013. https://philosiblog.com/2013/08/10/always-remember-you-have-within-you-the-strength-the-patience-and-the-passion-to-reach-for-the-stars-to-change-the-world/.

Arts, Health and Well-Being. Welsh NHS Confederation, May 2018. https://www.nhsconfed.org/-/media/Confederation/Files/Wales-Confed/Literature-review-of-arts-and—health-and-wellbeing.pdf.

Bradford, Sarah Hopkins. *Scenes in the Life of Harriet Tubman*. Auburn: W. J. Moses, 1869.

Clinton, Catherine. *Harriet Tubman: The Road to Freedom*. Boston: Little, Brown, 2004.

Darrow, George. *The Strawberry: History, Breeding, and Physiology*. New York: Holt, Reinhart, and Winston, 1966.

Davis, Julia. "The Yoke of Bondage: Christianity and African Slavery in the United States." https://www.youtube.com/watch?v=-qu8Rao9mrM.

DeFazio, Jeanne. *Keeping the Dream Alive: A Reflection on the Art of Harriet Lorence Nesbitt*. Eugene, OR: Resource, 2019.

DeFazio, Jeanne C., and John P. Lathrop, eds. *Creative Ways to Build Christian Community*. Eugene, OR: Wipf & Stock, 2013.

DeFazio, Jeanne C., and William David Spencer, eds. *Empowering English Language Learners: Successful Strategies of Christian Educators*. Eugene, OR: Wipf & Stock, 2018.

———. *Redeeming the Screens: Living Stories of Media "Ministers" Bringing the Message of Jesus Christ to the Entertainment Industry*. Eugene, OR: Wipf & Stock, 2016.

Douglass, Frederick. "Blessings of Liberty and Education by Frederick Douglass." 1894. Bartelby Research. https://www.bartleby.com/essay/Blessings-Of-Liberty-And-Education-By-Frederick-F38UG2TYA4PF.

Ellicot, Charles John, ed. *A Bible Commentary for English Readers*. Vol. 7. London: Cassell, 1906. Quoted from https://biblehub.com/commentaries/acts/17-26.htm.

Everett, Burgess. "Senators Duel over Race Card." *Politico*, May 23, 2014. https://www.politico.com/story/2014/05/jay-rockefeller-john-johnson-race-106983.

Flowers, Teresa, and Jeanne DeFazio. *How to Have an Attitude of Gratitude on the Night Shift*. Eugene, OR: Resource, 2014.

"Go Down Moses." *Wikipedia*. https://en.wikipedia.org/wiki/Go_Down_Moses.

Gudmestad, Robert. "Faith Made Harriet Tubman Fearless as She Rescued Slaves." The Conversation, December 3, 2019. https://theconversation.com/faith-made-harriet-tubman-fearless-as-she-rescued-slaves-127592.

"Harriet Tubman and the Underground Railroad (U.S. National Park Service)" https://www.nps.gov/articles/harriet-tubman-and-the-underground-railroad.htm

"Harriet Tubman Grave." *Wikipedia*. https://en.wikipedia.org/wiki/Harriet_Tubman_Grave.

"Harriet Tubman—I said to de Lord, 'I'm goin' to hold. . ." https://www.brainyquote.com/quotes/harriet_tubman_629150

"Harriet Tubman Strawberry Stroll Recommended for Harriet Tubman Day at U.S. Capitol." In "Latest News," *H.R. 1242 Resilience Project*. https://hr1242resilience.com/.

"Harriet Tubman Underground Railroad Visitor Center." *American Artifacts*, C-SPAN, May 26, 2017. Available online at https://www.c-span.org/video/?434005-1/harriet-tubman-underground-railroad-visitor-center.

"How Dr. King Cited the Constitution in His Mountaintop Speech." *Constitution Daily*, National Constitution Center, January 15, 2018. https://constitutioncenter.org/blog/how-dr-king-cited-the-constitution-in-his-mountaintop-speech.

Humez, Jean M. *Harriet Tubman: The Life and the Life Stories*. Madison: University of Wisconsin Press, 2004.

Janney, Rebecca Price. *Harriet Tubman*. Minneapolis: Bethany House, 1999.

Jordan, Elaine. "The Strawberry: A Symbol of Perfection and Righteousness." *Tradition in Action*, July 21, 2017. https://www.traditioninaction.org/religious/f035_Strawberry.htm.

"Martin Luther King, Jr.—We may have all come on. . ." https://www.brainyquote.com/quotes/martin_luther_king_jr_132359

"Numbers 21:4–9—The Bronze Serpent." *Enter the Bible*. Lutheran Seminary. https://www.enterthebible.org/Controls/feature/tool_etb_resource_display/resourcebox.aspx?selected_rid=549&original_id=24.

"Quotes." Harriet Tubman Historical Society. harriet-tubman.org/quotes/.

Shah, Rashiv, J., "Reflecting on Violence Against African Americans—The Rockefeller Foundation." 6/06/20. https://www.rockefellerfoundation.org/blog/reflecting-on-violence-against-african-americans/

"Signs and Symbols: Representing God and the Saints." *Catholic Tradition*. http://www.catholictradition.org/Saints/signs4.htm.

Spencer, Aida, B. and William, D. Christian Egalitarian Leadership: Empowering the Whole Church According to the Scriptures. Eugene: Wipf and Stock, 2020.

Spencer, Aida Besancon, and William David Spencer. "Responding to Floyd Killing: Creating Action Teams as Safeguards." *Applying Biblical Truths Today*, June 8, 2020. https://aandwspencer.blogspot.com/2020/06/responding-to-floyd-killing-creating.html.

"Structural Racism in America." Urban Institute. https://www.urban.org/features/structural-racism-america.

"Transcript of the Proclamation." National Archives online exhibit. https://www.archives.gov/exhibits/featured-documents/emancipation-proclamation/transcript.html.

Vryhof, David. "The Nativity of John the Baptist." Society of Saint John the Evangelist, June 25, 2013. https://www.ssje.org/2013/06/25/the-nativity-of-john-the-baptist-br-david-vryhof/.

"The Yoke of Bondage: Christianity and African Slavery in the United States." Harvard Divinity School exhibit, Andover-Harvard Theological Library, December 5, 2018—March 15, 2019. https://library.harvard.edu/events/yoke-bondage-christianity-and-african-slavery-united-states.

www.ingramcontent.com/pod-product-compliance
Lightning Source LLC
LaVergne TN
LVHW020313110826
845148LV00017BA/2649
* 9 7 8 1 7 2 5 2 8 4 7 8 4 *